WA

around

BETWS-Y-COED

Hilary Kendell B.A.
Hilary Bradnam B.Sc.

First Edition: May 1986
Second Edition: June 1988
Third Edition: January 1992
Fourth Edition: July 1998
Fifth Edition: March 2005

Published by Hilary Books
ISBN: 0-9533315-0-4

ACKNOWLEDGEMENTS:
We would like to thank all those who have helped us in the preparation of this booklet, especially Dave Whitmarsh, Dr and Mrs D.P. Howarth, Mr J. Parry-Evans, Justin Kendell and Andrew Davidson.

Since publishing the third edition, Hilary Kendell has died after a long illness. It was her wish that I should continue to publish the books so that more people may enjoy walking in this area.
Hilary Bradnam

Printed by Gwasg Carreg Gwalch, 12 Iard yr Orsaf, Llanrwst, Dyffryn Conwy.

Enquiries regarding sales:
Betws-y-coed (01690) 710741
e-mail: hilarybooks@aol.com

WALKS AROUND BETWS-Y-COED

(Bede house - prayer house - in the woods pronounced Betoos-er-koyd)

CONTENTS

LLWYBR CYHOEDDUS $\equiv$ PUBLIC FOOTPATH

Introduction

What do you do in Betws-y-coed?

One rewarding answer is **walk**.

This pocket guide describes a selection of walks around Betws-y-coed. Within a few minutes you can leave the noise of the main street and gain magnificent views of the mountains. The walks range from those taking less than an hour to all-day hikes. There are quiet strolls by the river and energetic climbs up the hillside. The walks have been chosen to include the most interesting features and best viewpoints in the area: you can choose between walks in the forest or in open farmland. All the walks are within the Snowdonia National Park. They do not follow coloured routes but where paths coincide, reference is made to them in the text. Where possible the walks follow old footpaths and tracks. Information about the region is included but kept separate from the directions.

All the maps are on the same scale in order that you can combine them as you wish and are sufficiently clear to use without an accompanying map. The most useful local map is the O.S. 1:25,000 Snowdonia National Park. All but one of the walks are loops so that you return to your starting point. Parking places are marked on the maps in case you wish to walk for only part of the distance. The times given do not include time taken to see places of interest. The distances given within the text are approximate, shorter distances being given in metres only.

Where it is advisable to go ahead of children e.g. on the approach to a waterfall or on an unavoidable road crossing, you will find an !

Stout shoes or boots are advised for all but a few of the local walks as all tracks may have muddy sections.

Remember the Countryside Code. Some warnings: avoid areas where forestry work is taking place for operators of machinery cannot hear you. No vehicles are allowed on Forest Enterprise roads without permission; old mines and quarries are dangerous. Dogs are unpopular everywhere, especially in the lambing season, so please keep them under close control. Don't forget that this is a working countryside.

Routes have been chosen to follow public rights of way or routes where use is permitted due to the goodwill of the Forest Enterprise or the Voelas Estate, but please do not use this book alone as justification for access.

Inns are marked on the map. Where the walk does not pass a place where refreshments are available you are advised in the text and the best picnic spots are pointed out.

This is a Welsh speaking area and Welsh place names are used where they are in general use. Paths and trackways have a special significance in Wales. They link isolated farms and cottages to bind them into a close community. They join together where people congregate e.g. at a school or chapel. Perhaps you will be following a track followed by Roman cohorts (page 41) or by drovers as they herded their livestock eastwards (page 68). It may have been used by packhorses carrying bales of cloth from the cottage industries to Llanrwst market (page 70) or by miners and quarrymen going to work in the hills (page 10). The Victorians created paths and drives from which to enjoy the local scenery (page 74) and some walks are in areas especially admired by Victorian artists (page 19).

By following these walks we hope that you will enjoy the scenery and obtain a glimpse into the rural life of the area, both past and present.

Since publishing the first edition we have realised what a changing countryside it is; wooden gates are replaced by metal ones, derelict cottages are renovated, road surfaces change. In subsequent editions we have adjusted the text where changes confuse the instructions but we have left it unaltered where the changes are obvious.

Please be aware that the Forest Enterprise may temporarily close footpaths in areas where felling is to take place.

We would be grateful for information about blocked paths or confusing changes and welcome comments and criticisms. Thank you for your compliments on the earlier editions.

Welcome to Betws-y-coed. Croeso i Fetws-y-coed.

KEY TO THE MAPS

——	Tarmac road
======	Track
- - - - -	Path
—+——+—■	Railway line with station
→	Route
～	Stream or river
◗	Lake
■	Building
▢	Ruin
♁	Church
P	Parking
⦂⦂⦂	Mine or Quarry area
⽊	Coniferous forest
♧ ♧	Broad-leafed woodland
✳	Viewpoint
km	Kilometre
✳	Place of interest

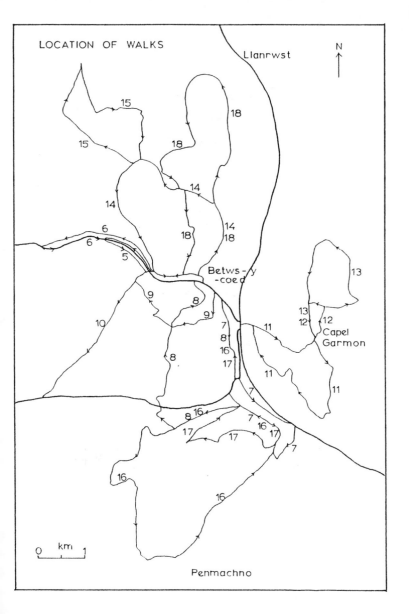

LOCATION OF WALKS

N

Llanrwst

15

15

18

18

18

14

14

6

6

5

14

18

14
18

Betws-y
-coed

9

8

9

10

8

7
8

16

17

13

13
12

12

Capel
Garmon

11

11

11

8

16

17

16

7

7

16

17

7

16

7

16

O km 1

Penmachno

7

Translation of some of the Welsh words used in this book

Afon – *River*

Coch – *Red*

Coed – *Wood*

Gwyn – *White*

Hafod – *Summer Dwelling*

Llyn – *Lake*

Mawr – *Big*

Pandy – *Mill*

Pont – *Bridge*

Pwll – *Pool*

Ty – *House*

Miners' Bridge Walk

This is a short walk following Afon Llugwy upstream to the well-known and unusual Miners' Bridge. The path passes through woodlands and fields, at first at the water's edge, but in its later stages rising gently above the spectacular gorge in which the river flows.

Time: ¾ hour   Distance: 3.5 kilometres/2 miles

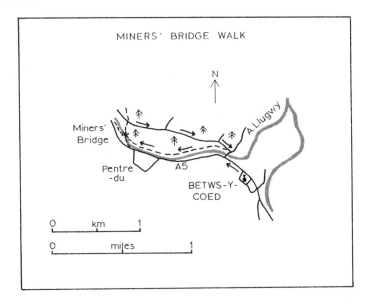

DIRECTIONS: Follow the A5 towards Capel Curig, and turn right over Pont-y-Pair.

Turn left, pass the car park, and immediately turn left again onto the footpath between the trees. The path keeps close to the river bank; follow it through the woods and enter the field by a stile. Cross this field, again keeping to the edge of the river, and after crossing a second stile the path re-enters woodland. The river banks become progressively steeper until you reach Miners' Bridge.

MINERS' BRIDGE

Miners' Bridge was built originally to provide a short-cut for miners living in Pentre-du who worked in the lead mines on the plateau to the north of the village. All the mines are closed now, but during the last century they provided considerable employment in the area. It is close to the place where the Romans used to cross Afon Llugwy on the Sarn Helen routeway (page 41).

There are three alternatives for the return route:

a) At the bridge turn right up the steep hill to the road, there turn right again to return to Pont-y-pair.

b) Cross the bridge and climb the steps opposite. Turn left along the path to the main road at Pentre-du, and turn left along the A5 back to Betws-y-coed.
c) Retrace your steps along the river.

This is an irregular 5 arched stone bridge crossing Afon Llugwy where the water plunges down the rocks into a deep pool below. The bridge is attributed to Howell Saer c. 1468, but the exact date of construction is uncertain, as is the date of widening on the upstream side.

The Smithy Walk

This is a short but steep walk, with a quiet atmosphere, giving a glimpse of the Betws-y-coed of 'days gone by'.

Time: 20 minutes   Distance: 1 kilometre/¾ mile

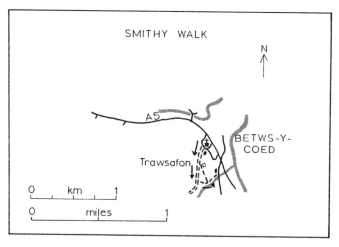

The walk starts from the road behind St Mary's Church (built in 1873 on land which was part of the village fairground). Take the track which leads uphill to the right of a stone bungalow. 200 metres from the entrance gate turn left onto a path which leads beside a ruined cottage, formerly Trawsafon.

A family of nine children grew up in the small homestead of Trawsafon. One of them became a famous local preacher, Robert Tomos, and Trawsafon became a nonconformist meeting place in Betws-y-coed in 1797. Bryn Mawr chapel was built in the village when congregations became too large to fit into the cottage. Trawsafon was still habitable at the beginning of the 20th century when it was the home of Arthur Owen, a blind harpist.

Follow the path (formerly a cart track) which fords a stream.

Below to your left, you will see the remains of a dammed pond which the stream fed to provide a constant supply of water for the village smithy.

Where the path joins another path, turn left. [If the stream is too full to ford, retrace your steps to the main track and continue uphill. Just before the track bends sharply to the right, leave it to turn left down a path. Cross a concrete bridge where a cascading stream flows over moss-blanketed rocks. The path then winds downhill to rejoin the route of the described walk.]

Turn left immediately before the large boulder, and continue down to cross a footbridge over the stream which spills out of the 'pond' in a series of waterfalls. The path continues down the slope through oak woodland native to Betws-y-coed.

As you approach the building you can see signs of the smithy to your right. There is a gap in the wall where the waterwheel protruded to be driven by the turbulent stream.

The path joins a road to the right of Betws-y-coed Motors. Turn left to reach the A5 and left again to return to St Mary's Church.

The River Triangle

This is a very easy walk on the level floor of the Conwy Valley. First it follows Afon Conwy to its confluence with Afon Llugwy, and then returning along the wooded banks of its major tributary.

Time: ½ hour   Distance: 2.5 kilometres/1½ miles

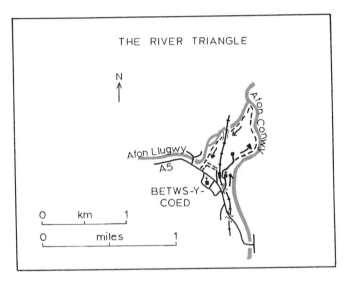

DIRECTIONS: From the A5 take the stone bridge over the railway line signposted to the Golf Club and St Michael's Church. Follow the road passing, on your right, Henllys Hotel, the old courthouse of the village. A few metres further on a path leaves the route to the right leading down to the suspension bridge over Afon Conwy. Continue along the road and enter the churchyard of St Michael's Church. The footpath continues along the right-hand wall above the river, but it is worth entering the church. (Key kept at Railway Museum and Tourist Information Centre.)

St. Michael's Church

St Michael's Church was built in the 14th century and was used as the parish church until tourism necessitated a larger one to be built in Victorian times. The nave and chancel are original but the north transept was added in 1843. At one time a gallery existed at the back of the church and this was used for the village school. There is a stone effigy of Gruffydd ap Dafydd Goch who used to live at Fedw Deg (page 76).

The font in St Michael's, showing intertwined leaves, is thought to be 13th century and may indicate that there was an earlier building there.

On leaving the church continue through the churchyard and rejoin the minor road. The road leads up to the Golf Club House, but at this point continue along the footpath on the river bank, entering the golf course by a kissing gate. Keep to the edge of the river as it meanders across the valley floor. Notice the remnants of old stepping stones in the river which can no longer be crossed.

Towards the far end of the golf course there is a long winding depression crossing the path which marks an old course of the meandering river. This is one of the first places where the river spills over its banks during times of floods. Flooding is a common occurrence in spring following rapid snowmelt in the mountains or after the all too frequent heavy rain!

The path continues to the confluence of Afon Conwy and Afon Llugwy. At this point the path turns left to follow back upstream along the banks of Afon Llugwy. The path enters a wooded area at a gate and continues under the railway line. It passes, on your left, Betws-y-coed Motor Museum, and, after a short distance, the Information Centre, before returning to Cae Llan (Village Green).

Clogwyn Cyrau Walk

This is a short but steep walk to a spectacular viewpoint on cliffs above Betws-y-coed. Most of the walk is on forest paths, but there is open moorland at the summit. It is well-worth the climb for the bird's eye view of the village.

Time: ¾ - 1 hour

Distance: 3 kilometres/2 miles

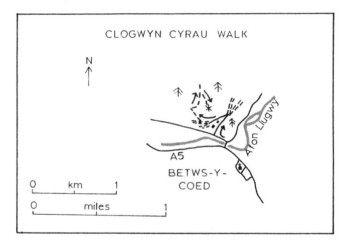

DIRECTIONS: Follow the A5 towards Capel Curig, and turn right over Pont-y-Pair, a stone bridge crossing Afon Llugwy. Turn left past the car park and take the first right up the tarmac hill. At the track junction, turn sharp left past the wood houses to the fork in the tracks. Here take the right-hand track uphill. After a further 50 metres turn right at a footpath sign up a path through the trees. At the junction in paths continue straight on, ignoring the 'Cyrau' signpost. Walk up this stony path, turning sharp right at a bench and sharp left 100m after. Cross one broken stone wall, and after 180 metres turn right (10m before the blue-topped post on your right) up a steep path to a rocky outcrop, covered in heather and gorse. ! Head towards the clump of conifers, and then pass through them to the cliff edge.

From this point there is a dramatic view down to the village about 600 ft/200 metres below. To your right are the houses of Pentre-du, with the mountains Moel Siabod, Glyderau and Carneddau beyond. To your left is the western end of Betws-y-coed and the Conwy Valley. Its rich agricultural land stands out in contrast with the poorer grazing of the Denbigh Moors beyond.

Return to Betws-y-coed by the same route.

Artists' Wood Walk

This is a beautiful walk alongside Afon Llugwy, returning through beech woodlands. It is so named after the many Victorian artists who frequented the area, inspired by the outstanding scenery. There are no steep sections on this walk.

Time: 1½ hours   Distance: 5.5. kilometres/3½ miles

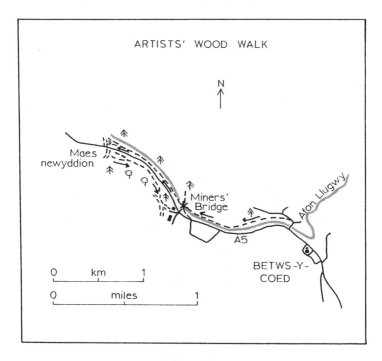

DIRECTIONS: **Riverside path:**   Follow the **MINERS' BRIDGE WALK** as far as the bridge itself. Cross the bridge and climb the steps, and immediately turn right along the path. Follow the path through the trees adjacent to Afon Llugwy. Along this stretch there are numerous places where it is possible to walk down to the river.

After 350 metres the path veers away from the river rising over a bluff. Cross a wooden bridge and after a further 350 metres, take the left hand fork, to continue to some derelict leadmine buildings, the mine entrance being visible on the opposite bank. Turn left up to the main road, and then left along the pavement for 40 metres. ! Cross the road.

Return route: Walk up the forest track signed Maes Newyddion and after 30 metres turn left along the narrow path. After 80 metres bear left through dense, young conifers. The route continues above the A5, skirting round a fence, and crosses a wooden footbridge among beech trees. Pass to the left of the Forestry Commission commemorative stone and cross two more footbridges. Continue through the woodland which becomes coniferous shortly before joining a track. Turn left on this track and follow it down to the A5. Here you can return to Betws-y-coed by turning right along the main road, or by crossing straight over, past the wooden barrier down to Miners' Bridge and returning as for the outward journey.

> *Probably the best-known of the many artists who were attracted to Betws-y-coed in the 19th century are J.M.W. Turner and David Cox. The latter came to stay here each summer from 1844 to 1856 staying mostly with the Roberts at the newly built Royal Oak Hotel. The sign board he painted for the Royal Oak (oil on wood) can be seen hanging above the fireplace in the reception area. It shows Charles II very well hidden in an oak tree at Boscobel.*

Swallow Falls Walk

This walk follows Afon Llugwy through trees upstream to the famous **Swallow Falls,** a spectacular waterfall even during a dry spell (2 miles west along the A5). This route passes **Miners Bridge** and **Ugly House** and has the added advantage of viewing the falls without paying! The path is rough in places and there are steep drops on the approach to the waterfall where care should be taken. It is inadvisable to take young children on the Swallow Falls path especially when the river is high.

For map, see page 22.   Distance: 9 kilometres/5 miles

DIRECTIONS: Follow the **MINERS' BRIDGE WALK** as far as the bridge itself. Here turn right up the steep path to the tarmac road. Turn left. After about 1 kilometre, ignore the path doubling back on your left, but take the next, rather indistinct, narrow path 50m later (30m before a track leaves the road on the left).

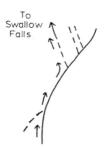

Ahead near the skyline on the opposite bank is a strange looking tree – a disguised aerial!

! The path winds down the **steep** slope which has been made into steps as it approaches the river. At the bottom the path crosses a stream by wooden platforms, the remains of a broken bridge.

The stream flòws through an old lead and zinc mine, the entrance to which can be seen on your right.

21

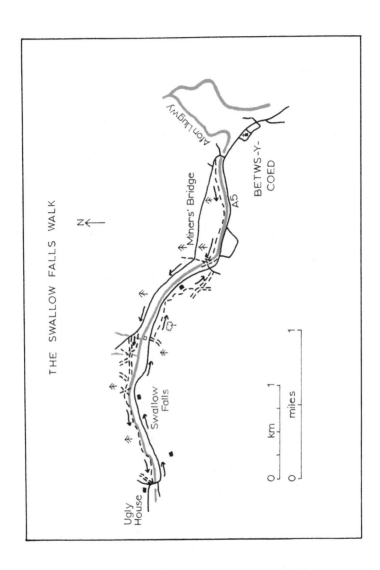

THE SWALLOW FALLS WALK

N

Ugly House

Swallow Falls

Miners' Bridge

A5

Afon Llugwy

BETWS-Y-COED

0 ___ km ___ 1
0 ___ miles ___ 1

The stream and rocks are discoloured because of the very high iron content of the water. Notice the stone supports either side of Afon Llugwy; originally these would have supported a tramway for carrying out the ore to the main road.

Continue along side the river for 170 metres to the next stream. Walk up the stream to a track. Turn left up the track, then fork left after 100 metres onto a path. The path turns left to cross a stream and soon rejoins the banks of the Llugwy. The path rises above Afon Llugwy as the gorge becomes progressively deeper, the path crosses another stream at a ford and is then joined by a track on the right. Shortly after there is a restraining fence on some of the steeper parts, but care should be taken on the next section. ! Swallow Falls soon comes into sight in the distance. Continue to the gap in the fence where there is the first observation point which can be reached by leaving the path. ! The second is 70 metres further on but is unprotected.

The original name of the falls was Rhaeadr Ewynnol, meaning Foaming Falls but this has been mistaken in the past for Rhaeadr-y-Wennol, meaning Swallow Falls, and the incorrect name is now used. It is said that the moaning of a local dignitary, Sir John Wynne, can be heard. It is claimed he has been condemned to purgatory in the falls since 1627!

From the second observation point take the path adjacent to the river continuing upstream, passing through woods and fields until a steep flight of steps by a stone bridge brings you on to the A5.

To your right is Ugly House (Ty Hyll) which is a supposed result of the loop hole in the local laws. It was said that if a house could be built between sunset and sunrise with smoke coming out of the chimney by dawn, then the builders owned the house. One wonders how such huge stones as can be seen in the walls were man-handled into position overnight!

TY HYLL.
THE UGLY HOUSE.

Turn left along the A5 over the bridge and follow the road (with pavement all the way), passing Swallow Falls Hotel where refreshments are available. This road leads back to Betws-y-coed but if you wish to leave the traffic, 600 metres beyond the hotel, turn right up a forest track signed Maes Newyddion. Here follow the directions for the return route of **ARTISTS' WOOD WALK** (page 20).

The Conwy Gorge, Fairy Glen, Conwy Falls and the Machno Falls

This is a walk following one of the loveliest stretches of water in the district as Afon Conwy falls over a series of rapids and waterfalls to the pool below Beaver Bridge (Pont yr Afanc). There are no steep hills to climb on this easy circuit. Allow plenty of time to explore **Fairy Glen**, see the **Conwy Falls, Machno Falls** and **Roman Bridge** and visit **Penmachno Woollen Mill.** The Conwy gorge remains virtually unchanged since its popularity in Victorian times and is very uncommercialized although a small charge is made to see the Conwy Falls and Fairy Glen. Be aware of the possible changes in the access to this walk due to widening of the A470.

For map, see page 26.   Distance: 11 kilometres/7 miles

DIRECTIONS TO FAIRY GLEN: Follow the A5 downhill from Pont-y-Pair, past the church and Post Office to take the minor road which turns right off the A5, to the right of the Cotswold Rock Bottom Shop. Follow it for 1½ km/1 mile through pleasant woodlands to Beaver Bridge. ! Take care where the railway bridge crosses the road.

PONT YR AFANC · BEAVER BRIDGE

25

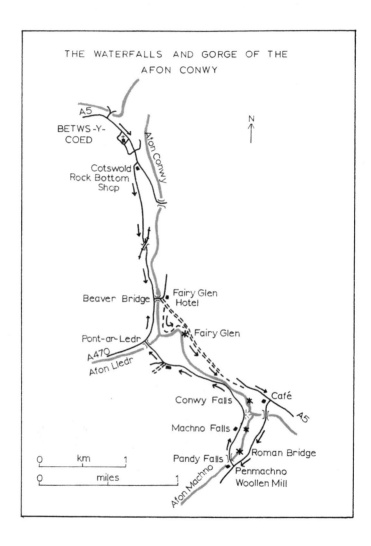

THE WATERFALLS AND GORGE OF THE
AFON CONWY

A5

BETWS-Y-
COED

Afon Conwy

N

Cotswold
Rock Bottom
Shop

Beaver Bridge

Fairy Glen
Hotel

Pont-ar-Ledr

Fairy Glen

A470
Afon Lledr

Café

Conwy Falls

A5

Machno Falls

Pandy Falls

Roman Bridge

km

1

Penmachno
Woollen Mill

miles

1

Afon Machno

Beaver Pool (Llyn yr Afanc) and Beaver Bridge (Pont yr Afanc). A wide welling pool where the river rests after its turbulent journey. It was not always considered a peaceful spot for the Welsh 'afanc' is more likely to refer to an aquatic monster than the likeable and docile beaver. Legends persist of the 'afanc' which was dragged in chains out of this pool by oxen and taken over Moel Siabod to be dropped into the 'bottomless' lake of Llyn-y-ffynnon-las.

Turn left over Beaver Bridge (! taking care as you cross the A470) and immediately turn right between the Fairy Glen Hotel and Beaver Bridge to follow the signed track. 80 metres after the car park, it is possible to make a detour to Fairy Glen through the gate on your right (Charge £1). The riverside walk follows the banks of the River Conwy to the confluence with the River Lledr. As you approach Fairy Glen, the sides of the gorge become higher. ! The slate steps may be slippery in wet weather.

FAIRY GLEN. FFOS NODDYN.

Fairy Glen, Ffos Noddyn. A famous 'beauty spot' best seen when shafts of sunlight beam into the deep ravine. The Welsh name Ffos (a ditch) and Noddyn (anoddyn – a chasm) gives a more dramatic impression than the sentimental Victorian name. When in flood the river bevels as it sweeps round the bends. A bridge across the ravine was swept away by floods.

THE WALK TO CONWY FALLS: Returning to the track, turn right for 1 km/¾ mile to reach the A5. At first this is a wide track which narrows into a path through woodland as it approaches the A5, muddy when wet.

The stone hut on the left hand side was the original booth for paying to visit Fairy Glen. Look carefully in the wall opposite and you can see where it has been filled in, blocking the Victorian entrance. This track was the old tollgate road on the London to Holyhead route and before that a packhorse trail. The oak trees which are seen on this unspoilt and peaceful walk are the remnants of the extensive oak forests of the upper Conwy Valley. To your right are views over the Lledr Valley towards Moel Siabod and to your left the rocky outcrop of Dinas Mawr.

As you follow the path through the wooded gorge you look down on the rushing and noisy waters of the Afon Conwy.

As you near the main road you will see the large blocks of masonry which Telford used to support his 'new' road built in 1815. In his diaries he describes this section as the most difficult of the route through the mountains.

! Through an opening join the A5. Carry on up the hill taking great care along this busy section of road for 150 metres to the Conwy Falls Café and the entrance to Conwy Falls.

Here the Conwy rushes into an amphitheatre-like hollow of strongly jointed Ordovician rock. The stream, stained brown by its journey through peat, is divided by a buttress of rock on which you can see the remains of an old salmon ladder which never worked. The new salmon ladder was completed in 1993.

TO THE WOOLLEN MILL AND ROMAN BRIDGE: From the A5 turn right to follow the B4406 for 1 km to the old Penmachno Woollen Mill.

Penmachno Woollen Mill was established in the 1830's as a 'pandy': a fulling mill where cloth woven on the local farms was brought by the farmers to be beaten under the fulling hammers (driven by a water wheel) to matt the fibres. The mill gradually expanded to include carding, spinning and weaving. It remained a family mill (Hannah Jones & Co.) until the 1960's when it was bought by Craftcentre Cymru. It has now closed.

Turn right (from the B4406) past the mill to cross the Machno river and Pandy Falls over Pont y Pandy. Look right to see 'Roman Bridge'. This narrow and lovely arch is probably a mediaeval packhorse bridge.

THE RETURN JOURNEY: **The Machno Falls:** Continue on the minor road over Pont y Pandy for ½ km to the Machno Falls. You will find them immediately opposite the second house on the left of the road 'Pandy'. (Notice the old potato clamp to the left of the house.) Almost hidden from the road, the falls are only a few yards away. ! Take great care as there is no fencing. Little known and uncommercialised, this is the best of the waterfalls!

An old guide book describes the falls as follows: 'Nature has doubly been assisted by art for the old mill wheel plays a most effective part in the view.' Sadly the wheel has gone but the shell of the old corn mill is still standing. The clear water of the Afon Machno is turquoise as it falls into the chasm and surges into the cleft below.

As you continue along the road there are several points at which you can get a view into the gorge. 100 metres from 'Pandy' there is a viewpoint which overlooks the rocky confluence of the Afon Machno and the Afon Conwy. Follow the road downhill for 1 km (ignoring the tracks which join from the left beyond Green Tub Cottage) to Pont ar Ledr. ! After crossing the bridge, turn right onto the A470 for ½ km.

To your right, behind the ruin of an old tollgate lies the pool of Llyn Tyn-y-cae where the Lledr joins the Conwy.

Before crossing Beaver Bridge, turn left to follow the minor road for 1½ km back to Betws-y-coed.

The Lledr Valley and Llyn Elsi Walk

This is a favourite walk which combines all the attractive features of the area following the meadows and sparkling waters of **Afon Lledr**. It climbs to the forested uplands around **Llyn Elsi**, returning along the **Jubilee Path**. The tracks are easy to follow and there is only one stiff uphill climb. ! A very dangerous crossing of the A470 at Gethin's Bridge is unavoidable. It is advisable to take your own refreshments: there are ideal picnic spots by the river and the lake.

For map, see page 33.   Distance: 11 kilometres/7 miles

DIRECTIONS: **To Pont ar Ledr** – From Pont-y-Pair, follow the A5 downhill, past the church and the Post Office. Take the minor road which turns right off the A5 to the right of the Cotswold Rock Bottom shop and follow it for 1.5 km/1 mile through pleasant woodlands to Beaver Bridge. ! Take care where the railway bridge crosses the road. ! At the road junction turn right along the A470 for ½ kilometre to Pont ar Ledr.

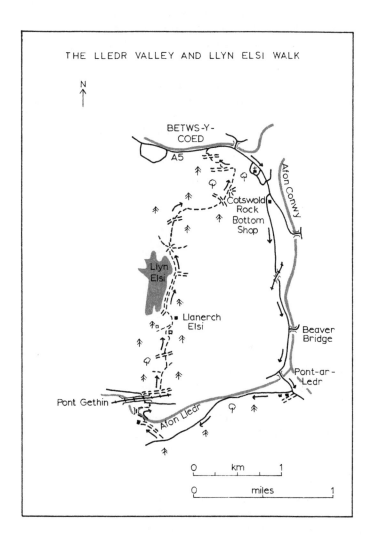

THE LLEDR VALLEY AND LLYN ELSI WALK

N

BETWS-Y-
COED
A5

Afon Conwy

Cotswold
Rock
Bottom
Shop

Llyn
Elsi

Llanerch
Elsi

Beaver
Bridge

Pont-ar-
Ledr

Pont Gethin

Afon Lledr

| 0 | km | 1 |

| 0 | miles | 1 |

This two-span 15th century bridge once carried the main road to Penmachno. It is thought to have been built by the same mason, Howell Saer, who built Pont-y-Pair in Betws-y-coed.

The Valley Road: Turn left over Pont ar Ledr to follow the minor road uphill. Take the first turn right in front of two houses (Gilfach and Tan-yr-Allt). Continue along the road which parallels the Afon Lledr with views of Moel Siabod in the distance for 1½ kilometres. Notice Giant's Head (see page 66).

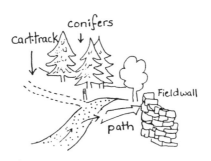

The path to the river

Where the road rises over a slight hump and trees replace fields on your right, turn right to follow a field wall towards the river along a rough path. Past a gate the path widens to a grassy track with a steep slope to the river on your right. The track continues through deciduous woodland over a single span bridge towards a farm. Where the track curves left to approach the farm (75 metres beyond the bridge) turn right between high stone gateposts to follow a path which is paved with large stones as it nears the footbridge. The modern wooden bridge sits on old foundations; the original bridge was destroyed by a falling tree. The path curves to the right to reach stone steps to the main road 100 metres to the right of Gethin's Bridge.

Gethin was a local builder of great repute who also built St Mary's Church in Betws-y-coed. The massive viaduct seems far too imposing for the single line diesel it carries today.

To Llyn Elsi: ! Turn left under Pont Gethin and immediately right up the drive marked 'Craig Lledr' for 60m, to where, almost opposite the last bridge turret, a path leads uphill to the left, marked by red paint on the rocks.

A stiff climb up the hillside follows. There are good views over the Lledr Valley to admire while you get your breath back. As you near the brow there is a small flight of concrete steps and the slope becomes more gentle. Ignore the faint path which joins from the left but continue straight on keeping the stream to your left. 70 metres further on, the path turns left, off the main trackway, to cross a wooden footbridge into a grove of deciduous trees. The path crosses a forest track and continues as a roughly paved path through coniferous forest over fairly level ground to a ruin.

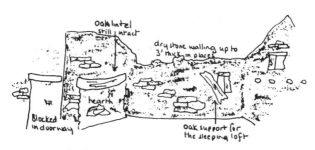

A glimpse inside the ruined cottage
near Llanerch Elsi in 1986.

Walk around to the front of the cottage and continue in the same direction up the slope to a stream, ignoring a path joining from the left. 50 metres further on, bear left (you can see the chimneys of Llanerch Elsi through the trees to your right). Initially the path is bordered by a field wall on the right. At the corner of the wall, keep to the main path. Where you emerge from the trees, turn right onto a forest track beside the lake. Llyn Elsi used to provide the water supply to Betws-y-coed. After 400m the track turns right, away from the lake. At this point, a well defined footpath continues along the lakeside: follow it to the monument.

From this viewpoint you can see many mountains of Snowdonia. On the left is Moel Siabod, the next mountain block includes the Glyders and Tryfan (three peaks) and finally the peaks of the ridge to the right are the Carneddau.

The return to Betws-y-coed along Jubilee Path: With your back to the inscription take the path, slightly to your right, leading away from the lake (marked by green paint). Cross straight over the track taking the path which bears to the right. Continue along this well-defined path through a mixture of forest and woodland. Cross straight over at the next track after which the path becomes quite steep. ! There are vertical drops to your right and at several places there are spectacular viewpoints over Betws-y-coed and the Conwy Valley. As the path levels out, it passes through a small cutting. 20 metres later bear right down the footpath to the next track. Turn left and then take the next right down the path which becomes steps as it approaches the A5. Turn right along the road to return to the village centre.

The Llyn Elsi and Hafod-las Walk

This upland walk incorporates forest, woodland and farmland; it passes **Llyn Elsi** with spectacular views of the mountains, and crosses the old slate quarry of **Hafod-las**. It returns on **Sarn Helen**, a Roman road. The first part is steep, but once the lake has been reached the walk is flat or downhill. It can be extended by combining it with the **SARN HELEN WALK** (page 41).

Distance: 5.5 kilometres/3½ miles

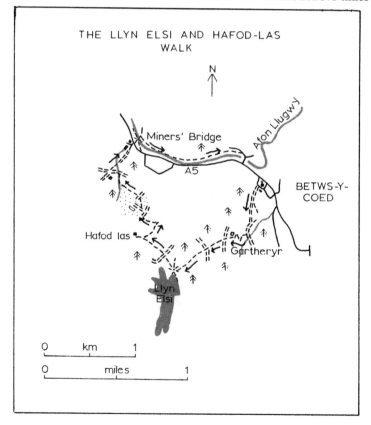

DIRECTIONS: From the A5 take either road uphill beside St Mary's Church and turn up the track to the right of the modern bungalow. After about 600 metres, at a standing stone, turn right on a well-defined path which crosses the stream by a wooden bridge. This path zig-zags up the steep slope to the top of the crags. At the top, the path flattens and passes a ruined cottage called Gartheryr on your right.

In 1749 a Calvinistic Methodist came to live in Betws-y-coed and weekly meetings were held in Gartheryr. The congregations grew to such a size that famous Welsh preachers came to visit the cottage.

Continue along the gentler path, crossing straight over at two tracks. As you leave the trees, Llyn Elsi comes into view. Continue on to the monument.

At this point you can see many of the mountains of Snowdonia (but not Snowdon!). On your left is Moel Siabod; the next upland area includes the Glyders and Tryfan (three peaks), and finally the right-hand ridge comprises the Carneddau.

With your back to the inscription, take the path slightly to your left downhill. After 100 metres, where the stony path sweeps left, bear right along a narrow muddy path, through an area of small birches, to a track, and cross straight over. Continue along this path, then cross a fence by the stile, where there is now a wall to your right and a fence to your left. Continue along the path until shortly before Hafod-las cottage a grassy track doubles back to the right adjacent to some old machinery. Turn along the track with a wall on your left. Continue down this winding track until you reach the barn. Here turn sharp left along the track skirting the top of the field.

Enter the woodland and Hafod-las quarry by a stile. Follow the wire fence on your left until the track turns sharp right. Here there is a view into the quarry.

Continue on the track downhill. Just after the wall on your right becomes a fence, turn left along the level path which leads towards the quarry buildings. ! Do not enter any ruins or clamber on the spoil heaps.

Hafod-las quarry is a small slate quarry which was operative mainly in the 19th century. The quarry workers lived in Pentre-du, directly below, or in Rhiwddolion, an isolated and now deserted village on Sarn Helen, the Roman Road (page 43).

Walk along this old tramway to the gate. Just before the gate turn right down a narrow path. This narrow path leads steeply downhill to the right partly hidden by tree branches to a small stream which comes out of an adit. Cross the stream and continue past two small ruined buildings.

There are spoil heaps on either side; notice the difference in the stones comprising them. On your right are huge blocks from the initial quarrying whereas on your left are split slates which are reject roofing tiles.

Keep close to the right of the second building and just beyond it the path drops down to an old inclined tramway. Turn right onto the tramway, then immediately turn left over the fence into the field at the stile.

Cross the field keeping to the base of the spoil heaps on your left. Continue to the far end where there is a stile leading into woodland. Cross the fence and follow the narrow path through the many fallen trees towards a stream and follow the path down to a track. Turn left and walk along the track for 100 metres to crossroads.

At these crossroads if you require a longer walk turn left and turn to the **SARN HELEN WALK** (page 41) and follow the directions from the asterisk.

To return to Betws-y-coed, turn right down the path, crossing a bridge and a stile, then a gate and continue down to the main road. Here you have the choice of following the road or the riverbank. For the former, turn right down the A5. For the latter walk, cross straight over, pass the wooden gate and follow the path down to Afon Llugwy.

Cross Miners' Bridge and turn right along the river bank back to Betws-y-coed.

To look for:
Walls which keep in the cattle
but allow the sheep to roam.

Sarn Helen Walk

This is a linear walk following the course of a **Roman road** from the Llugwy Valley over an undulating plateau into the Lledr Valley. There is an initial uphill climb, but once the top of the plateau has been reached, it is a gentle walk through forest and moorland, passing the deserted village of **Rhiwddolion**.

The return journey can be made by train on the single track railway from Pont-y-Pant to Betws-y-coed. There are train timetables at Betws-y-coed Station or phone 08457 48 49 50. Be warned – Pont-y-Pant is only a halt so trains do not stop there without being hailed!

For map, see page 42   Distance: 7 kilometres/4½ miles

DIRECTIONS: Take the **MINERS' BRIDGE WALK** (page 9) as far as the bridge, cross it and continue straight up the path to the A5. Cross straight over and take the road ahead keeping the row of houses on your right. The path soon rises steeply uphill crossing a gate, a stile and a footbridge before reaching crossroads in the tracks. Again, continue straight over.

* Pass the cottage on your left (the route is occasionally marked by blue paint). Here the path is very steep and is often deeply rutted by streams which flow down it during heavy rain. Keep on up to the next crossroads at a gate and go straight over.

> *This path follows the route of the Roman road, Sarn Helen, which led from Caerhun in the north down to Trawsfynydd in the south during the Roman occupation. Parts of the path on sloping ground are on embankments, still clearly visible, although now the original stonework is obscured mostly by soil, as is the road surface.*

Continue up the hill past the white farmhouse, through a gate beyond which the track is sunken below ground level. As you pass a gate on your right you can see down the hill to the first of the deserted cottages and the now renovated chapel. After a few metres at a fork in

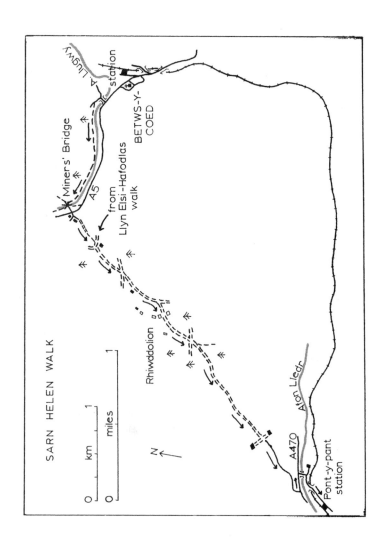

SARN HELEN WALK

Miners' Bridge

from Llyn Elsi-Hafodlas walk

Rhiwddolion

BETWS-Y-COED

station

Afon Llugwy

A5

Afon Lledr

A470

Pont-y-pant station

N

km 0 1

miles 0 1

42

the tracks, take the more distinct right-hand track downhill which swings round to Rhiwddolion through a gate. To the left and right are ruined cottages; a public footpath leads in front of the right-hand terrace and it is worth exploring down there. ! It is unsafe to enter the buildings.

These houses are the remains of a scattered hamlet which was inhabited until the 1930's when the closure of the local mines and quarries forced people to move to find other employment. Fruit trees can still be seen growing in the old gardens giving an evocative atmosphere to the place. Many have now been renovated as holiday homes.

Return to the path which continues uphill through rougher ground. As conifers close in on your left, the gradient flattens. At a gate there are trees on both sides for a short stretch after which you cross straight over at a forest track.

A few hundred metres later, a gate leads on to moorland where views are obtained of the hills to the south. At this point the path begins the descent into the Lledr Valley 500ft/150 metres below. At 2 more gates continue straight on, passing a house on your right, after which the route becomes a tarmac road. Continue down to the main road, and turn left for 200 metres. Turn right over the river signed to Plas Hotel and Pont-y-Pant Station, then turn right again at the far side of the bridge. This road brings you to the station, about 400 metres further on.

Capel Garmon and the Neolithic Tomb

After an initial climb up the valleyside, this is an easy and pleasant walk on a rolling upland plateau to the east of the Conwy, where, unimpeded by trees, you can enjoy wide views of Snowdonia. In a landscape of small farms and in a region of early settlement there is plenty of interest, especially the **Neolithic Burial Chamber** to the south of **Capel Garmon**. Walks beyond Capel Garmon are described on pages 52 and 54.

To return, you can choose between a) following the edge of the upland plateau or b) descending into the Conwy Valley to see **Conwy Falls** and returning via **Fairy Glen**. Paths may be muddy in winter.

Distance: 10 kilometres/6 miles

For map, see page 45.

DIRECTIONS: **To Capel Garmon:** From Pont-y-Pair follow the A5 downhill, past the Church and the Post Office, continuing across the Waterloo Bridge to the Ty Gwyn Hotel.

The Waterloo Bridge, 'the Iron Bridge', is constructed entirely of cast iron. It was built in 1815 to carry Telford's London to Holyhead road. It is decorated with the national symbols, the rose, the leek and the thistle.

You will find the path to the left of the Hotel. Steps help you to climb the first part of what is obviously a very old track. Cross a forestry track and continue upwards to join a tarmac drive. Turn left along the drive for 40 metres, then turn right through a gap in the wall. Cross a track, climb over a stile and follow the footpath through a copse for 150m. Cross the stile over a gap in the wall into a field by a telegraph pole. Follow the left hand boundary stepping over a low dividing wall and fence to follow the path uphill. Continue until you reach the track to Gelli Lynnon Farm but do not enter the farmyard. Instead, turn right through the edge of the trees, crossing the next rough track, to an old stone stile to the left of the field gate. The path

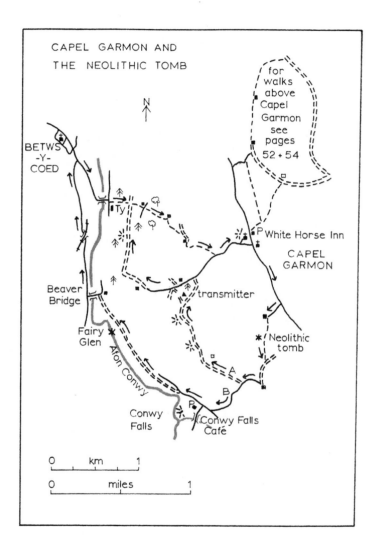

CAPEL GARMON AND
THE NEOLITHIC TOMB

for
walks
above
Capel
Garmon
see
pages
52 + 54

N

BETWS
-Y-
COED

Ty

P White Horse Inn

CAPEL
GARMON

Beaver
Bridge

transmitter

Fairy
Glen

* Neolithic
tomb

Afon Conwy

A

B

Conwy
Falls

P

Conwy Falls
Café

0   km   1

0   miles   1

across the field is not very clear but keeping to the left you will soon see a kissing gate ahead. This is a good spot at which to relax and enjoy the view westwards to the mountains.

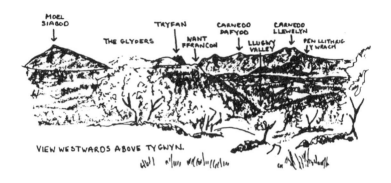

VIEW WESTWARDS ABOVE TY GWYN.

The path becomes clearer after the gorse bush, continuing ahead over rough pasture with patches of bare rock. Keep the low stone wall to your left and, as a wall joins on your right, walk up the rise to join a farm drive. Turn right and pass through the farm yard at Pant y Pwll. These are kennels, so don't worry about the dogs barking. Passing between the house and the barn, bear right through a small iron gate to the left of a stone outbuilding. The path now curves left to cross a wooded gully, crossing the stream over stone slabs and climbing upwards to a stepped stile. Cross an area of rough pasture, keeping a wall to your right and you will soon see the village of Capel Garmon in the distance to your left. The track is muddy as it crosses a stream. A large boulder to the right of an open gateway (and stile) marks the way into the next field. Cross this field heading for the roof of the farm building ahead.

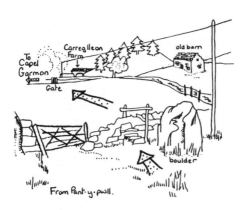

From Pant-y-pwll.

Turn left onto a tarmac track for ½km to Capel Garmon. (If you wish you can leave the track at the base of the hill before it reaches the village, turning left over a stepped stile to climb the slope to reach the rear of the church. The view is splendid. Cross the next stile and follow the wall to the kissing gate.) The tarmac track joins the main road opposite a chapel. Turn left if you wish to walk into the centre of the village to the White Horse Inn and the walks described on pages 52 and 54 or right to continue the walk to the Capel Garmon Neolithic Tomb.

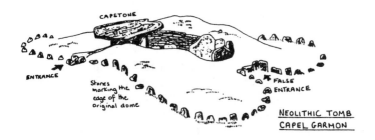

NEOLITHIC TOMB
CAPEL GARMON

To the Capel Garmon Neolithic Tomb. ! From the road junction by the chapel turn right to follow the road for ¾ km/½ mile to a sign marked 'Ystafell Gladdu Capel Garmon Burial Chamber'. Welsh Black cattle are reared in this area. Look ahead and take evasive action where necessary! Turn right along the track to Tyn-y-Coed which lies in a dell to the right. Where the farm track curves to the right to enter the farmyard, take a signed footpath leading through a gate along the fence to a second gate. You will now see the tomb (surrounded by fencing to protect it from cattle) towards the left of the adjoining field.

> *The Capel Garmon tomb was built about 5,000 years ago as a communal burial ground for the local people. (There is another 2 miles to the N.E. of Nebo: 'Maen Pebyll'.) Originally it would have been a smooth, long mound of earth (a long barrow) 94' long and 42' at its widest. Today stones mark the edges of the former mound. Inside all the three chambers would originally have been capped by large stones but only one remains. The tomb has a false entrance; the two horns of the mound gave the impression that the entrance was on the east side, whereas a hidden entrance led from the south. In the middle of the last century it was used as a stable and in 1924 work was done to prevent it deteriorating any further.*

To Penrhyddion Farm: Keeping to the left of the tomb, cross the stile, leaving the knoll to your left and follow the footpath signs which point to the left over an area of rough pasture. They point to a kissing gate. Climb up a slight rise, keeping a wall (and the view!) to your right until you meet a farm track. Turn right along this muddy track to the diversion sign.

Walk diagonally down the hillside to follow the fence on your right hand side. Cross the stile and turn right down the road for 200m to where it enters rough pastureland through a gated opening.

This is decision time for you can, if you wish, return via the Conwy Valley in which case see page 50 or follow the edge of the upland to rejoin the track to Ty Gwyn.

A. The return route following the edge of the upland. Turn right onto a cart track which climbs steadily through an area of rough pasture past the ruins of Tyn-y-gerddi. To your left you look beyond the hump of Dinas Mawr into the Machno and Lledr valleys, while ahead in the west is Moel Siabod. Ignore the first gate in the wall to your left, but go through the second and third gates in front of you.

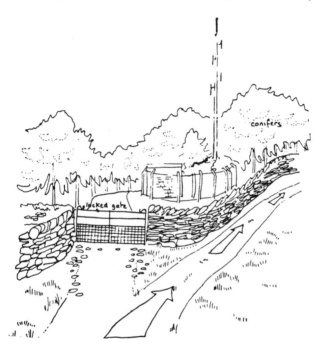

Where the track is seemingly blocked by a locked gate alongside a radio transmitter bear to the right to follow the path which hugs a wall (on your left) bordering forested land. The path leads to a gate opening onto a patch of rough grazing adjoining a tarmac road. Turn left along the road, passing on your right the single storey building of Cefn Rhydd. Continue down the road to the farm track of Tan-y-Bwlch.

Continue ahead and as you round the bend you will see Tan-y-Bwlch on your left known to local people as the home of the late gamekeeper 'Bob' whose 'white' horse would bring him back faithfully from the White Horse Inn. Fork right along the forestry road (which is barred to vehicles) for 1½km/¾ mile. Ignore the track leading to the right beyond Tan-y-Bwlch and the one which descends the slope to your left as you round the spur. As you near Betws-y-coed, you will have a 'bird's-eye' view in a felled area.

Where electricity lines join the track, turn left to follow the steep path bordering a wall to join the A5 to the right of the Ty Gwyn Hotel. ! Cross the busy A5 and continue over the Waterloo Bridge to Betws-y-coed.

B. The return route via the Conwy Valley: Continue along the track from Penrhyddion farm through a caravan site to the A5. ! Cross the busy A5 to Conwy Falls Café and the entrance to Conwy Falls (details: page 29). ! Follow the A5 downhill for 150m. The road is very busy and there is no footpath. Leave the road at a gap which is the entrance to the old road (replaced by Telford's road in 1815). It is now a path through woodland with views of the Conwy in a deep gorge to the left.

George Borrow travelling along the old road in 1862 describes this section. 'At length I came to a steep mountain gorge down which the road ran nearly due north, the Conway to the left running with great noise parallel with the road amongst broken rocks which changed it into foam.'

The path widens to a safe and peaceful track with views over the Lledr Valley towards Moel Siabod to the left and the crags of Dinas Mawr rising to your right. Beyond the fifth gate is the entrance to Fairy Glen (see pages 27 & 28).

'An immense mountain on the right of the road particularly struck my attention and on enquiring of a man breaking stones by the roadside, I learned that it was

called Dinas Mawr or the large citadel perhaps from a
fort having been built upon it to defend the pass . . . '
George Borrow, Wild Wales 1854.

The track continues downslope to join the A470. To return to the centre of Betws-y-coed turn left over Beaver Bridge and immediately right to follow a minor road following the river to your right. ! Take care where a railway bridge crosses the road.

Walks above Capel Garmon:
The Capel Garmon Triangle

This is a short walk up the ridge above Capel Garmon to gain fine views of the mountains with very little effort. It is an ideal pre or post lunch sortie or can be combined with the walk from Betws-y-coed (page 44). The downhill track has a very rough surface so stout shoes/boots are essential.

Distance: 2 kilometres/1½ miles

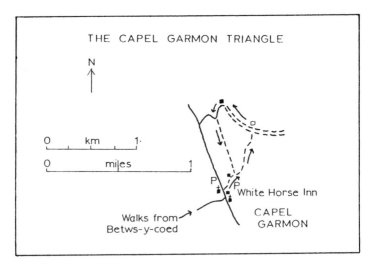

THE CAPEL GARMON TRIANGLE

N

km   1·

miles   1

White Horse Inn

Walks from
Betws-y-coed

CAPEL
GARMON

DIRECTIONS: **To Pen-y-Ffridd**. Take the road which leaves the main road to the left of the car park immediately before the White Horse Inn. Pass the Public Lavatories and turn left along a concrete path in front of a row of bungalows. Pass through a kissing gate and follow the right hand boundary of the field for 50m to a white farmhouse. Turn right to follow the right hand field boundary. Cross a stile to the left of a gate and bear left following a path (to the right of telegraph poles) which gradually climbs the slope for 100m to a second stile. Keep left at the base of a gorse-covered slope to another stile. The path continues through a larch grove and you will already be able to enjoy views of the mountains.

When you come to an open field at the top of the hill continue along a path in the same direction as the electricity wires until you reach the corner fence-post, to the right of which is a kissing gate. Go through the kissing gate and keep to the left hand boundary of the field (avoiding the marsh) to join a track by the dramatically damaged hafod of Pen-y-Ffridd.

(Return to p.55 for the 'Walk Around Moel Trefriw'.)

Pen·y·Ffridd

Turn left down the steeply sloping old track, etched into the hillside by generations of use, to Gwninger.

The return route to Capel Garmon: Opposite the farm of Gwninger the track swings left and descends into the valley through a gate. As it rises it turns sharply to the right. At the angle of the turn, leave the tarmac track to go through a gate onto a field track. Continue straight ahead at the base of a dell through two more gateways and over a stile. When crossing the last field head towards the gate 50m to the left of the farm buildings but turn right down the track of your outward journey. Retrace your route to Capel Garmon.

Walks above Capel Garmon:
Around Moel Trefriw

A walk on the uplands above Capel Garmon around the **northern slope of Moel Trefriw** to obtain splendid views down the Conwy Valley. After an initial uphill climb to the crest of the ridge the gradients are very gentle. A very pleasant walk in open country. It can be combined with the walk to Capel Garmon from Betws-y-coed (page 44).

Distance: 5 kilometres, 3 miles

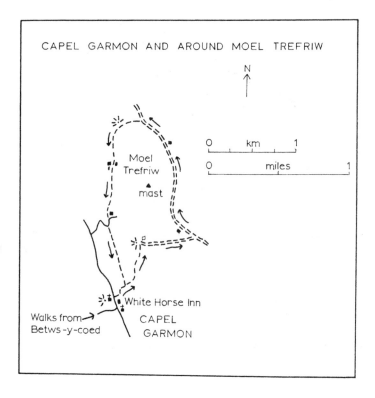

CAPEL GARMON AND AROUND MOEL TREFRIW

N

Moel
Trefriw

▲
mast

O   km   1

O   miles   1

White Horse Inn

Walks from→
Betws-y-coed

CAPEL
GARMON

DIRECTIONS: From the rear of the White Horse Inn, Capel Garmon follow the directions to Pen-y-Ffridd given on page 52.

From Pen-y-Ffridd turn right (away from the view) to follow a level track for over ½ km/½ mile, passing through one gate and ignoring the track on your right. Turn sharp left to the farm of Bryn Rhug. The track passes between the farm and barns to your left and low corrugated iron sheds to your right. Immediately past the farm the track is very muddy but beyond a stream and gate it improves. Continue downhill along this track for approximately 1½ km/1 mile until, just beyond the first bends on the track, you reach a kissing gate on the left.

The road from Nebo to Llanrwst follows the ridge on the far side of the deep valley to your right. This was the old stage-coach route from London via Pentrefoelas and Nebo to the bridging point at Llanrwst.

The path you are now to follow keeps to the same height as it loops round the northern shoulder of Moel Trefriw. There are splendid views to your right. Passing through the kissing gate you will see another gate ahead leading into the following field. You have to walk ahead over a slight rise before the next gate is visible. Beyond it, the path widens into a grassy track which hugs the right hand boundary fence. The track is shaded by trees as it approaches Belmont. At Belmont the public footpath passes through the farmyard, although at the time of going to print there is no stile in the fence. When you reach the house do not take the drive leading to the right but continue ahead, passing between a fence to your left and a barn and glass building to your right, to a kissing gate. The public footpath crosses the next field to a gate midway along the opposite hedge (skirt the edge of the field if there are crops or long grass growing and don't forget to shut the gate!). The path crosses the next field to pass to the right of the farm of Gwninger through two gates to join a surfaced track. Turn downhill to follow it. You may wish to follow this tarmac track to the road turning left for ½ km to the village or follow the footpath which leaves the track at the point of the bend, back to Capel Garmon (described on page 53).

The Gwydyr Forest Walk:
Southern Loop

This circular walk involves a strenuous uphill stretch at the beginning to **Llyn Parc** but the rest involves fairly gentle walking on the **Nant Plateau** through forest and rough pasture before returning to the valley bottom. Several lakes are passed en route and on clear days there are many spectacular view points. It can be extended to an all day walk by combining it with the **GWYDYR FOREST NORTHERN LOOP** (page 61).

For map, see page 57.   Distance: 9.5 kilometres/5½ miles

DIRECTIONS: Leave the A5 at Pont-y-Pair. At the far end of the bridge turn left, past the car park, and take the first right up the steep tarmac road. Follow this road as far as the hairpin bend to the left, and leave the road to take the upper of the two forest tracks. This track continues uphill along the side of the Conwy Valley for about 500 metres, but as it starts to drop down take the well-defined path on your left (marked by yellow and white topped posts) which rises still higher. This path leads through the trees and eventually reaches the Aberllyn Gully, now scarred by the remains of leadmining from the last century. Cross straight over at the junction of footpaths, ignoring the path joining from the right. The route becomes progressively steeper till it reaches the top of the gully where the slope becomes gentle, and the path follows the side of the stream until you reach Llyn Parc.

> *This lake has been used as a reservoir in the past for water power for the mining below. Since the mining ceased, the dam has been broken deliberately following a flood and as a result the water level of the lake is now kept low. The deep greenish colour is due to the high mineral content of the water, e.g. lead, zinc and copper.*

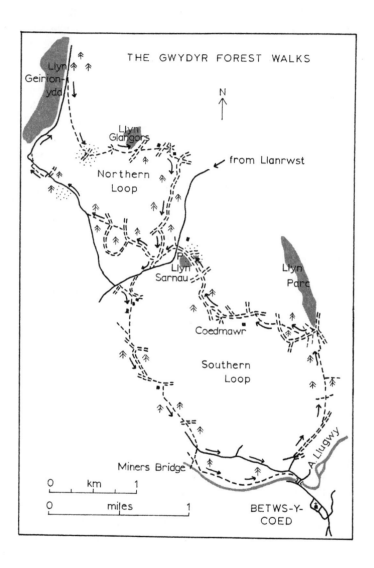

THE GWYDYR FOREST WALKS

N

Llyn
Geirion-
ydd

Llyn
Glangors

← from Llanrwst

Northern
Loop

Llyn
Sarnau

Llyn
Parc

Coedmawr

Southern
Loop

A. Llugwy

Miners Bridge

0   km   1

0   miles   1

BETWS-Y-
COED

At the lake turn left along the forest track. Ignore the two cycle tracks on your right, but after about 150 metres turn right along a footpath just before the track sweeps left. Cross straight over at the next track and continue along the path until you join another track. Turn left along this track ignoring the track to the right which leads up the side of the old dam wall. This track remains level for a while, passing Coedmawr on your left, which used to be a small-holding.

As the track starts to go downhill (ignoring the path to the right) there is a spectacular view of the mountains of Snowdonia ahead of you. About 100 metres beyond this, there is a dramatic exposure of volcanic rocks – a part of a lava flow which erupted beneath the sea over 400 million years ago. At the junction in the tracks, turn right uphill. This track winds between trees and farmland with minor tracks joining and eventually crosses Llyn Sarnau (dries in summer). Just beyond the lake, the track joins a public road.

Here are the remains of one of the many leadmines in the area. The lead ore was exploited in the 19th century and now most of the old workings are derelict. The buildings here have been converted into an outdoor education centre, but the original smelter chimney still towers over it. The spoil can be seen lying in heaps around, and throughout the walk you will see many fenced-off mine shafts.

Turn left through the car park, and scramble up the steep stony path. The path continues on the level and then joins a track. Turn left here and continue for about 150 metres to the next junction.

If you are combining the southern and northern loops, turn to the northern loop directions and continue from the asterisk (page 62).

* Turn left at this junction, and within a few metres you reach the road. Turn right here and continue along the public road for 400 metres until you reach more mine workings on your left. Turn left at the signed path about 50m before the turning to Llyn Geirionydd. Cross straight over the gravel track and, with the fence on your right, follow the path to the stile.

You are crossing more mine workings here. If you jump off the stile you will feel the ground vibrating indicating it is hollow beneath!

Hafoty pencraig

Cross the field and head to the gap in the wall ahead. Cross the stile and bear right slightly uphill to a wooden signpost. Walk to the right of the restored barn and head for the farm (Hafoty Pencraig). Cross the stile, and keeping the farm buildings on your right go through the gap in the wall. Bear left diagonally down the hill, skirting just to the right of the small rocky knoll and head for the stile to the right of the trees. Cross the stile and keep left downhill through a boggy area to a track. Climb over the stile and turn left along the track. Within 50 metres you reach another stile, cross this, bear left at the path junction and take the right hand track which is becoming rather overgrown. Continue until this track reaches a field, cross the stile and follow the remnants of a track across the field. As you cross the brow of the hill, head towards the barn of Diosgydd Uchaf. Join the track which leads between the farmhouse and the barn, pass to the right of the barn, and after 10 metres turn right down a narrow path signed by a blue topped post.

Follow this path down between walls to a ladder stile. Cross this and the path re-enters the forest. The first few metres are very steep, but the path soon becomes a gentle gradient for 800 metres, crossing straight over at a rough forest track and eventually reaching the road.

The return to Betws-y-coed can be either along this road to the left, or down the very steep path opposite, to Miners' Bridge and left back along the near river bank.

The Gwydyr Forest Walk:
Northern Loop

This is an upland walk across the **Nant Plateau** passing several lakes including **Llyn Glangors, Llyn Sarnau** and the largest in the forest, **Llyn Geirionydd**. Parts of the walk are through forest, but much is through pasture, and although the route is undulating there are no steep sections.

It can be reached by walking the **GWYDYR FOREST SOUTHERN LOOP** (page 56). Alternatively drive along the A5 to Waterloo Bridge and turn left along the A470 to Llanrwst. After 6 kilometres/4 miles you reach the town of Llanrwst, and here turn left over the narrow stone bridge. At the far side of the valley, turn left and immediately right up the hill signposted to Nant-Bwlch-yr-Haearn. This road rises steeply for 2 kilometres/1½ miles to the hamlet of Nant-Bwlch-yr-Haearn, and just beyond is parking space by Llyn Sarnau. Start the walk there.

Distance: 7.5 kilometres/4 miles

For map, see page 57.

DIRECTIONS: Turn your back on the lake, cross the road, and take the steep stony path up the hill opposite.

Below are the remains of one of the many leadmines in the area. The lead ore was exploited in the 19th century and now most of the old workings are derelict. The buildings here have been converted into an outdoor pursuits centre, but the original smelter chimney still towers over it. The spoil can be seen lying in heaps around, and throughout the walk you will see many fenced-off mine shafts.

Follow the path through the forest, until you reach a track. Turn left here and continue for about 150 metres to the next junction.

* Turn right, and continue straight on at the next junction past the cottage on your right. About 50 metres beyond the building, turn left down a stoney path through the trees. (At the time of going to print, the trees are being felled and the path has been destroyed. It should be restored after felling.) Cross straight over at the next track and continue down to the public road. Turn right along the road, and continue for 600 metres passing lead spoil heaps on your left. About 100 metres after the forest closes in again a forest track joins the road on your right. Turn left opposite this track down an indistinct grassy path and cross the stream. Turn right along this levelled path which is the remains of an old tramway leading from the leadmine. At the fence turn right uphill back to the road, and turn left down the road. Just before the right hand bend, it is safer to walk on the right hand verge, following the path parallel with the road. Once this path rejoins the road, Llyn Geirionydd comes into view.

Walk along the road beside the lake to the second gate where the forestry begins. Just before the gate, turn sharp right on a path which doubles back up the hillside. As the path rises through bracken there are spectacular views in both directions over the lake, and towards the top there are glimpses of the mountain summits on your right.

The path leads to more mine workings; cross the stile and turn left between the fences. Turn right through a gateway to walk between the spoil heaps to an old ruin, and drop down on to the track.

Ahead telegraph wires lead up over the grassy hill, straight ahead and between the two rows is a stile. Cross this stile, and follow the left-hand wires up the field to the next stile, pausing to look back at the mountains behind.

Cross this second stile and continue in the same direction over two ridges as the path bears right to Llyn Glangors. Cross the old dam by a stile, climb the ladder stile and follow the path up to a track. Cross straight over here and continue up the path. Cross the stile leading onto moorland and follow the broken wall on your left to pass to the right of the cottage. Cross the next track using the stiles which are staggered slightly to the left and after the second stile aim for the highest point, slightly to your left. The stone base of a trig. point comes into view – this is a good place to rest.

This point is at 1012 ft/307 metres and there are good views in all directions. The main mountains of Snowdonia are visible behind you and ahead is the rich agricultural land of the Conwy Valley with the bleak Denbigh Moors beyond.

From the trig. point, take the path slightly to your right downhill to the wall. Turn right along the wall to a stile. Cross the stile and carry on down the path to crossroads. Turn right on the track and continue for 1 kilometre/¾ mile. At the next junction turn left by a small lake. Continue along this track for 700 metres to the next junction.

If you are combining the southern and northern loops, turn to the southern loop directions and continue from the asterisk (page 58).

Otherwise, turn left at this junction, and within a few metres you reach the public road. Turn left and shortly you return to Llyn Sarnau.

The Gwybrnant Walks

A walk along quiet roads and forestry tracks in the less frequented area south of the Afon Lledr to explore the secluded valley of **Gwybrnant** (valley of the viper). There is plenty to see and do. **Ty Mawr** is famous as the birthplace of Bishop William Morgan who translated the Bible into Welsh. There is a nature trail behind the house and **pony trekking at Ty Coch**. There are spectacular viewpoints to climb to if you wish but otherwise there are only two uphill sections.

You can return a) along a forestry road or b) extend your walk into the **Machno Valley** (a detour to Penmachno is possible) returning via the **Conwy gorge**.

Distance:

a) Shorter route – 14 kilometres/9 miles
b) Longer route via the Machno Valley – 18 kilometres/12 miles

For map see page 65.

It is advisable to take your own refreshments or make a detour to Penmachno.

! The peace of the area is shattered on certain days of the year when car rallies pass through certain sections of the forest. There is usually one in November, one in February and one in March. There are no summer rallies. The Tourist Information Bureau can advise you of the dates in advance.

DIRECTIONS: **The Walk to Gwybrnant**. Follow the directions to Pont ar Ledr given on page 32. Turn left over this 15th century bridge to follow a minor road up the slope. Take the first right turn at a junction of routes to follow the lowest road which parallels the Afon Lledr in front of two houses (Gilfach and Tan-yr-Allt). It is not much used in winter but be aware of traffic in the summer.

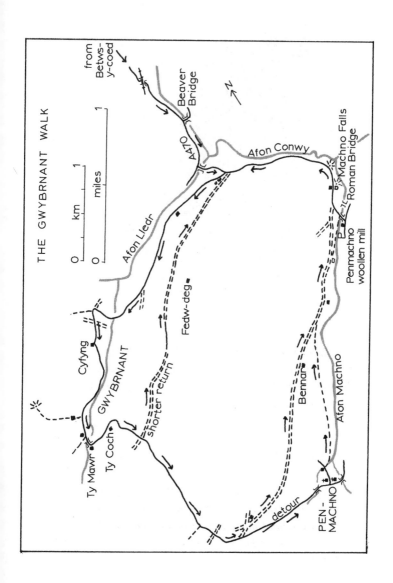

THE GWYBRNANT WALK

from Betws-y-coed

Beaver Bridge

N

A470

Afon Conwy

Afon Lledr

Machno Falls

Roman Bridge

Penmachno woollen mill

km

miles

0   1

0   1

Fedw-deg

Cyfyng

GWYBRNANT

shorter return

Bennar

Afon Machno

Ty Mawr

Ty Coch

detour

PEN-MACHNO

65

GIANTS HEAD

As you approach a row of cottages, look back at the cliffs towering over the Lledr to see why it is called Giant's Head. The Welsh name is Clogwyn y Gigfran – cliff of the raven.

The road continues into the Gwybrnant. For 2½ km/1½ miles from the road junction it follows the base of the slope, at first bordering the valley pastures and then rising through woodland and forest. At a junction of routeways it turns sharply left to climb into Gwybrnant.

Cyfyng was the school and chapel which served the local community. In the 1940's there were 40 children attending school here, some walking from as far as Llyn Elsi. The desks were converted into pews for the Sunday services.

CYFYNG

The Gwybrnant. There is a change in the landscape as you reach the gentler slopes of the valley left 'hanging' as the Lledr Valley was deepened by glaciation. Continue to follow the gated road on the valley floor. (If you wish to make a detour to obtain views of the mountains climb the track behind Tan-y-Clogwyn, the building up the slope to your right.)

Beyond Pwll y Gath a path from Dolwyddelan enters the Gwybrnant. Cross the Afon Wyber to reach **Ty Mawr**, now a property of the National Trust. There is a signed nature trail from Ty Mawr.

The sturdy cottage of Ty Mawr is famous as the birthplace of William Morgan (c.1540-1604) who first translated the entire Bible into Welsh. After spending his childhood in Gwybrnant he studied Greek and Hebrew at Cambridge and became bishop of Llandaff and later of St Asaph. His translation, published in 1588, had a great effect on the Welsh language, for in effect he established a 'standard Welsh' from the many local dialects. Ty Mawr is open to

*the public most days from Easter to October but check
with Tourist Information first.*

The road bears left and up the slope passing on the right Ty Coch a pony trekking centre. Ty Coch is open all the year: prior booking is advisable.

*You are following a 'drovers' road'. In the 16th century
cattle were more important than sheep in the hills and the
small black Welsh cattle (together with ponies, pigs and
geese often all shod for the journey) were driven in herds
of 500-600 beasts along routes which kept to the lonelier
uplands on their way eastwards to the English markets. In
1587 William Morgan joined their noisy company to
travel in safety to take his manuscript to London.*

The Return Journey. a) Shorter Route. Continue up the hill from Ty Coch for ½ km. At the first crossroads turn left onto a forestry track. Keep to the main track **downhill** for about 3 km/2 miles to bring you back to the road junction. Turn left to Pont ar Ledr. Turn right onto the A470 and left before crossing Beaver Bridge to retrace your route to Betws-y-coed.

b) A longer Route via the Machno Valley. Continue past Ty Coch (carrying straight on at the crossroads) for approximately 1½ km/1 mile. The road crosses a forested plateau and winds down into the Machno Valley (if you wish to make a detour to Penmachno see page 70 although the return can be muddy after heavy rain). As the road begins to descend more steeply look for a stone post on your right with a broken post signing a path to Dolwyddelan. Continue along the road which bends sharply to the left and crosses a forestry track. Round the next corner look for a forestry road on the left which is barred to traffic (see map). Turn left to follow it for 150 metres before turning right at a crossroads of tracks at Pentop farmhouse.

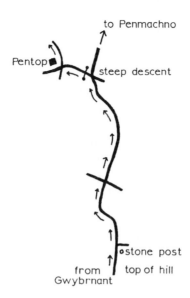

to Penmachno

Pentop

steep descent

stone post

from
Gwybrnant

top of hill

The main forestry road follows the base of the wooded slope for 4 km/2½ miles to a tarmac road. There are good views over Penmachno and the gentle slopes of the Machno Valley where the track reaches the edge of the forest.

> **Viewpoint:** *At Penmachno houses cluster around the 'Pont Llan' over the Afon Machno. It is a very old village: tombstones kept in the church are the earliest Christian tombstones in Wales (A.D. 540). They indicate a settled community here using a Roman system of government after the Romans had left (one local man is described as a 'magistratus'). In late mediaeval times it became a focus for the drovers' routes. The noisy herds crossed the bridge and followed the 'Ysbyty Road' which you can see climbing the slope on the far side of the village. In the 19th century slate quarried further up the valley at Cwm Penmachno brought prosperity.*

[**Detour to Penmachno.** Continue downhill on the road from Ty Coch bearing left at a road junction to enter the village. The church key is kept at the nearby farm of Tyn-y-ddôl. There is an inn, the Eagles. To return to the route of the walk, take the road which leads towards the river between the church and the chapel, past the recreation ground. Cross the bridge over the Afon Glasgwm and turn right through the gate opposite the farm of Tyn-y-ddôl. Turn left immediately before a second gate and go through the kissing gate at the far end of the field. Turn left along the track. At Blaen-ddôl, cross the stile and walk straight ahead across three fields to the track between Bennar and the road. Turn left up the track for 25m, then turn right through a gate to continue along the valley fields.

120m past the white house up on your left, go through a gate, then turn left along the wall. Turn right along the old road between wall and fence for 200m to a stile on your left. Take the path up to the forestry track and turn right.]

Halfway along the track you pass the solid and imposing 16th century farmhouse of Bennar. There are more 16th and 17th century farmhouses in the Machno Valley than in any other comparable area of Gwynedd. At that time the Machno Valley would have been a bustling rural community with an income not only from farming but from the thriving woollen industry. The women at Bennar would be busy carding, spinning and weaving or knitting stockings. The hard wearing cloth was taken by cart or packhorse along the old road to the woollen markets at Llanrwst or across the valley to market towns to the east.

The forestry road has displaced the old road which followed roughly the same route. It is possible to join the old track in places. It is very muddy but the peaceful, timeless atmosphere is worth the effort.

One such place is approximately ¾ km/½ mile beyond Bennar. The trees on the right give way to fields. Continue along the forestry track for a further 400m and look for a ruin amongst trees at the base of a slope to your right. 30m further on clamber down a short bank and cross a broken fence to join the old road. Turn left to follow it, keeping between a wall and the forestry fence, ignoring other exits. You will soon hear the river to your right and see the weir and old mill. As the fence and wall veer right, continue straight ahead through the fence. The track continues over a rocky hump to join the tarmac track at Pont y Pandy.

Whether you have followed the old or new roads turn left at the junction with the tarmac road for your return journey. (Turn right if you wish to visit Roman Bridge first, see pages 29 and 30).

Just a few yards opposite the second house on the left (Pandy) you will find the lovely Machno Falls. ! Take care as there is no fencing (see page 30 for details). 100m further on there is a viewpoint overlooking the rocky confluence of the Machno with the Conwy. The road continues for a further 1½ km/1 mile to Pont ar Ledr. Turn right to retrace your route to Betws-y-coed along the A470, turning left immediately before Beaver Bridge.

Panorama Walk

A walk on the south western side of the Conwy Gorge to enjoy some of the finest views in the district. It is a walk for the more dedicated rambler as it involves a stiff clamber up a forested hillslope and some of the tracks have a very rough surface. It follows the Conwy gorge before turning to join for a short distance the Victorian Panorama Walk at Coed y Ffynnon. The walk continues up the hillside to join a forestry road commanding fine views before descending on a mediaeval track 'the path of Gruffydd ap Dafydd Goch'.

For map, see page 73.   Distance: 12 kilometres/8 miles

DIRECTIONS: **Following the gorge of the Conwy.** Follow the directions from Betws-y-coed to Pont ar Ledr on page 32. Turn left over Pont ar Ledr to follow the tarmac road uphill, bearing left at the junction with two roads from the right, to continue in front of Green Tub Cottages. This road runs alongside the Conwy gorge and there are views through the trees into the rocky ravine. There is a small 'layby' on the left approximately 1½ km/1 mile from Pont ar Ledr with views looking down on the rocky confluence of the peat-stained Conwy and the clear waters of its tributary the Machno. 100 metres further on, opposite the first detached house, 'Pandy', on this road, you will find the Machno Falls. These lovely falls are only a few yards to the left of the road. ! Take care as there is no fencing. (Details on pages 30 & 31.

The way to Coed y Ffynnon and Panorama Drive. Continue along this road for a further 200m to where a forestry road, bordered by beech trees, leads off to the right. Turn right to follow this road for 270m. Round the first bend, before a junction of forestry roads, there is a trackway leading off to the right through the trees: the entrance is marked by two rough stones. Fork right to follow this unmade track for 150m to a gate leading to a clearing. The path keeps to the right of the rough pasture to meet a well-marked cart track. Turn right to Coed y Ffynnon.

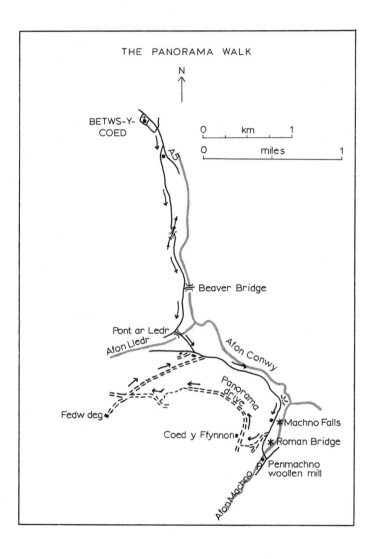

THE PANORAMA WALK

N

BETWS-Y-COED

km

miles

Beaver Bridge

Pont ar Ledr
Afon Lledr

Afon Conwy

Panorama drive

Fedw deg

Machno Falls

Coed y Ffynnon

Roman Bridge

Penmachno
woollen mill

Afon Machno

There is a religious aura about this lovely old house and the area surrounding it. Somewhere here (perhaps on the same site) was a mediaeval chapel. People came to be cured by the 'healing waters' of the well and a large stone 'maen siglo' – the shaking stone, in the forest nearby, was said to shake when the church bells rang. The house dates from the 16th century and was used for a time in the 17th century as a nunnery. Inside, a royal coat of arms indicates that it was the home of one of the Welsh princes. On the right hand side of the porch there are the remains of an ecclesiastical window.

The track continues in front of the house and past the boundary wall to become **Panorama Drive**.

Panorama Drive was constructed when Lord Banks, a Lord Chief Justice, used Coed y Ffynnon as a shooting lodge at the beginning of the 20th century. At that time Lord Banks and his guests enjoyed magnificent views of the Conwy Valley as they drove along in their pony and trap but today the view is partly screened by trees and the drive itself comes to a 'dead end'.

Continue along Panorama Drive to the end. Carry on along the footpath straight ahead. The path dips at first and crosses a stream before winding up through trees to the forest track.

Turn right along the forestry road. As you round the brow of the hill there is a fine view of Moel Siabod and, as the road descends in a series of bends, the view widens to a true panorama, in a recently felled area.

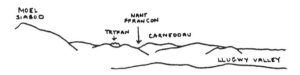

The return journey via the path of Gruffydd ap Dafydd Goch.

Continue down the slope following the forestry road until you meet a junction of tracks just past the barrier. Turn right at a sharp angle to descend the hill on a rutted track, (the track leading left climbs to the farm of Fedw Deg). This rough track to the bottom of the hill is a mediaeval track known as the path of Gruffydd ap Dafydd Goch.

> *Gruffydd ap Dafydd Goch was a knight of royal blood, a great nephew of Llywelyn. He fought for the Black Prince in the French Wars of Edward III. He lived at Fedw Deg on the hillside above and it was down this track that his body was carried for burial at St Michael's Church, Betws-y-coed where there is a fine stone effigy (see page 15). He was a very large man and his last journey was evidently a cumbersome one to be remembered.*

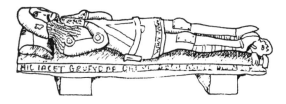

The effigy of Gruffydd ap Dafydd Goch c.1380
St Michael's Church

At the base of the hill, turn left in front of Green Tub Cottage, continuing downhill to Pont ar Ledr. ! Turn right onto the A470 and left before Beaver Bridge to retrace your route to Betws-y-coed.

A Walk via Llyn Parc towards Llanrwst

A walk via Llyn Parc to follow the side of the Conwy Valley towards Llanrwst returning up the Nant valley and over the upland plateau. It follows good dry tracks for most of the way excepting for one muddy section and has only two uphill stretches. It is possible to shorten the walk by continuing to Llanrwst and returning to Betws-y-coed by train. Train enquiries – telephone 08457 484950.

For map, see page 78.   Distance: 13 kilometres/8 miles
                    Distance to Llanrwst: 7½ kilometres/4½ miles

DIRECTIONS: Follow the directions on page 56 as far as Llyn Parc.

At the lake, bear right following the track for 350m to a crossroads. Turn right to walk downslope. Ignore the path leading to the right but continue along a level track for 175m before bearing right to walk downhill. As this track steepens, it curves to wind downhill along an old embanked track through a section known as the Drws Gwyn leading to a long straight track.

After 1½ km/1 mile, fork right alongside the newly created Bowling Green, ignoring both the path on your right and the rough track forking left. Continue along this forestry road for 1¼ km/¾ mile. Gwydyr Uchaf, now the headquarters of Forest Enterprise, lies approximately halfway. You will see a track leading to it branching off to the right.

> *Gwydyr Uchaf was much larger when it was built in 1604 with extensive formal gardens. The private chapel (built in 1673) has a remarkable ceiling and is well worth a visit. The key is available from Gwydir Castle on the road below.*

Continue past the car park to a staggered crossroads. (In order to visit the Grey Mares Tail Waterfall cross straight over at the crossroads and walk for 150 metres before looking back to your right.)

[DETOUR. To Llanrwst. At the crossroads turn right, walking

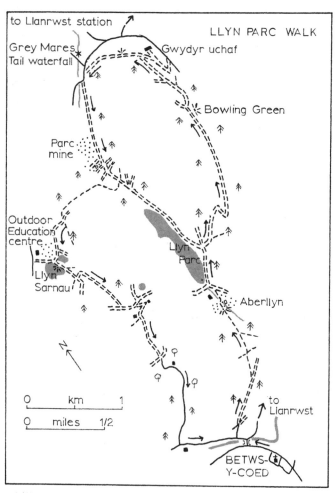

LLYN PARC WALK

to Llanrwst station

Grey Mares
Tail waterfall

Gwydyr uchaf

Bowling Green

Parc
mine

Outdoor
Education
centre

Llyn
Parc

Llyn
Sarnau

Aberllyn

N

0   km   1

0   miles   1/2

to
Llanrwst

BETWS-
Y-COED

downhill for ½ km/½ mile. At a road junction turn left and immediately right for a further ½ km to Llanrwst.]

From the crossroads turn left to walk uphill for 50m before bearing left, to follow a barred tarmac road for 1 km/¾ mile. At first it rises only gently between a forest plantation and the smooth pastures of reclaimed spoil heaps but then climbs steeply up the forested slope.

Mining at the Parc Lead Mine continued into the 1960s. The channelled stream is stained red by the ores in the old workings. (See the Information board.)

Ignore the two tracks which cross the road and continue to climb the now grit-surfaced road.

(If you wish to shorten the walk, continue on the road uphill. It soon levels out and reaches Parc lake. Retrace your steps to Betws-y-coed.)

200 metres past the second track, turn right along a wide path.

Follow it for 50m before it narrows after crossing more waste.

Keep to the path as it passes through the next undulating section which is bordered by fenced-off old mining shafts. The path levels out and becomes an enjoyable walk through forest for 1 km/½ mile.

After a short stony rise the path continues ahead through mature trees for 75m before bearing left through a gap in a broken wall. It rises gently to join a forestry track.

Turn right along this main track. Rounding a bend it passes behind the chimney of the old Llanrwst lead mine. Ignore a track on your left opposite a gate, but continue to the next junction to turn left across Llyn Sarnau causeway. At the next crossroads in tracks, turn left, then immediately right. Walk uphill passing a white bungalow from where you can view the mountains. The track descends to join a forestry road where you turn left for 125m. Fork right down the track and after going through the gate, turn immediately sharp right.

On reaching the front of Coed Mawr, ignore the stile ahead and bear left. The track now winds through a patchwork of pastures before re-entering forest. Ignore the track on your left and go through the gate into trees. Cross straight over at a crossroads and continue downhill for 1½ km/1 mile to a road junction. Turn left for ¾ km/½ mile to return to Pont-y-Pair.